PENGUIN BOOKS

THE SPACE BETWEEN MEN

Mia S. Willis (they/them) is a poet, popular educator, and cultural historian from Charlotte, North Carolina. Their work, twice nominated for the Pushcart Prize, has been featured by *The Slowdown*, *The Shade Journal*, *Palette Poetry*, *The Offing*, *the minnesota review*, *Homology Lit*, *NarrativeNortheast*, and others. Willis has earned fellowships from Cave Canem, La Maison Baldwin, The Watering Hole, Lambda Literary, and Chashama's ChaNorth. A two-time Best of the Net nominee, they are the author of *monster house.* (Jai-Alai Books, 2019), the 2018 winner of Cave Canem's Toi Derricotte & Cornelius Eady Chapbook Prize.

Also by Mia S. Willis

monster house. (Jai-Alai Books, 2019)

The National Poetry Series was established in 1978 to ensure the publication of five collections of poetry annually through five participating publishers. The series is funded annually by Amazon Literary Partnership, William Geoffrey Beattie, the Gettinger Family Foundation, Bruce Gibney, HarperCollins Publishers, the Stephen and Tabitha King Foundation, Padma Lakshmi, Lannan Foundation, Newman's Own Foundation, Anna and Olafur Olafsson, Penguin Random House, the Poetry Foundation, Amy Tan and Louis DeMattei, Amor Towles, Elise and Steven Trulaske, and the National Poetry Series Board of Directors.

THE NATIONAL POETRY SERIES
WINNERS OF 2023 OPEN COMPETITION

the space between men by Mia S. Willis
CHOSEN BY MORGAN PARKER FOR PENGUIN

Field Guide for Accidents by Albert Abonado
CHOSEN BY MAHOGANY L. BROWNE FOR BEACON PRESS

Post-Volcanic Folk Tales by Mackenzie Schubert Polonyi Donnelly
CHOSEN BY ISHION HUTCHINSON FOR AKASHIC BOOKS

The Sky Was Once a Dark Blanket by Kinsale Drake
CHOSEN BY JACQUELINE TRIMBLE FOR UNIVERSITY OF GEORGIA PRESS

Playing with the Jew by Ava Winter
CHOSEN BY SEAN HILL FOR MILKWEED EDITIONS

the

space

between

men

Mia S. Willis

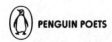 PENGUIN POETS

PENGUIN BOOKS

An imprint of Penguin Random House LLC

penguinrandomhouse.com

Pages 59–64 constitute an extension of this copyright page.

Set in Granjon

Designed by Sabrina Bowers

LIBRARY OF CONGRESS CONTROL NUMBER: 2024014891

ISBN 9780143138105 (paperback)

ISBN 9780593512203 (ebook)

Printed in the United States of America

1st Printing

to the birth fam:
thank you for keeping me tethered to this life.

to the earth fam:
i'm just tryna get like you.

CONTENTS

1. articulation.

2. semantics.

3. contact.

1. articulation.

Like love: first you pick up; then you lay down; then discard; then discard; then discard.

That's love. Right?

SAMIYA BASHIR

the giant's causeway.

a kwansaba for my right hand.

i believe in god the way [right]
hand does not think before it claps
my faith be an open palm / spread
out wide and yet still [right] here
still clement / still trying to say her
own name [right] / still praying for the
bravery to call herself a deity too

THE DUKE OF YORK @ 5 PM.

for mickalene thomas.

men talk about the weather like they were born for it.
      or it was born for them.
          whichever.

a bar feels like an unsavory place to write until
      i hear two men talking about the weather like a femme noire
      they unlearned how to love.
        i hope she stays this beautiful.
        i hope we get lucky.

and suddenly, i must write nature an apology.
      make it sound like "ain't no mountain high enough,"
        like "give me the night."

i apologize the way only a fellow femme noire can.

    first.
    often.
    for the men and their climate change conversations.
    aware that forgiveness is buried somewhere in the atlantic
       and archaeologists are coming for that too.
    familiar with all we will have to surrender before they let us rest.

after safia elhillo.

a kwansaba for my jaw.

i smile too wide in every photo
my jaw a canal or a femme
the way they know "open" means "empty"
and still they split anyway / my jaw
means "border in gender country" / see:
"jaw line in the sand" / see: "force
of both the river and the dam"

razbliuto (between sozopol & nessebar).

when my mother tells me *eggs are laid to be broken*
OR
my heart churns my skin shea butter smooth
OR
a glass of rakia scares the depression back down my throat

my mother always says
you do not know what you do not know
but instead i hear
the world is waiting on the other side of your eggshell
do not be afraid to birth yourself beautiful

and so my heart and i equally yoked in our daring
let tenderness pool in the creases of this flesh map
watch the goosebump roads rise to greet the mercy

it is an ode to the way life has cracked this body open
the way love clings fiercely even to the jagged breaks
every breath a meditation on remaining
                                        here.

A DESCRIPTIVE GRAMMAR ABOUT GENDER.

a. "boy" and "boi" are homophones distinguishable only by their context.

    ex. police officer to my father: *where are you coming from, boy?*

    ex. lover's hand to my cheek: *where are you coming from, boi?*

b. the sequence of sounds [trænz] is both a prefix and adjective that appears before the word it describes.

    ex. the swahili name for the transatlantic slave trade is the "maafa." the "catastrophe."

    ex. there is no swahili word for "transgender."

    there was no need to name the sources of the salt in the seawater before the "catastrophe."

c. "femme" and "fem" are homophones distinguishable only by their context.

    ex. diamonds are a femme's best friend.

    ex. my fem is a home for the bloodiest hands.

d. lexical semantics demonstrate that "body" and "gender" are historically synonymous.

    ex. *this is my body which is broken for you.*

    ex. take this gender in remembrance of me.

BOI FINGERS.

after dennis r. rush of the pine plains writing group.

i'll come right out and tell you what this poem is about.
i know that's what you're looking for.
this poem is about the time my father called me
JAMES
for an entire summer when i was six
simply because i asked him to.
how my father was the first to reach for these boi fingers
and say *I WILL ALWAYS CALL YOU, NO MATTER THE NAME.*
the way he taught these clumsy digits the difference between soil and dirt.

the body ballet.

a bop.

i sit upright in my bed under spring sunrise.
say the daily prayer that this body's choreography—
with all its black and arabesque,
with all its queer and assemblé—
does not send me tumbling to the earth
or the orchestra pit of an early casket. first position.

i was cast in this role but no one taught me how to dance.

the curtain rises on me at a breakfast table. voices in the house say *black first*. développé.
my black body slouches into the chair.
eats the bacon. the eggs. the slurs. the chocolate jokes.
devours both the ripe and the rotten attention.
my queer body has been dining in the wings for years. échappé.
licks the grease from the plate before it disappears backstage.
is told to call this empty stomach intermission so the principal can breathe.
i stand en pointe between them, suspended animation. second position.

i was cast in this role but no one taught me how to dance.

and here we are. act after act. hunger after hungry. penché.
these bodies with their / my fingers gripping shoulders and silverware.
i quiver on the barre between them as the sun spotlight moves.
does the audience know what it is to long for the decrescendo into silence?
what to call the pouring of their / my blood from a gravy boat?
the season of rebirth? horace fletcher? a phoenix with broken wings? third position?

i was cast in this role but no one taught me how to dance.

APOTHEOSIS OF THE BLACK BOI.

a landay for the changing hand.

rilke says *god is more gessoed wood*
than painter's fingers so we icons rename ourselves.

here we stand, ritual half-complete
halo ungilded / rib cage aflutter with prayers

stumbling over mirror liturgy
shade the jaw / stress the brow / conceal the chest / stay alive.

damp roskrish spines bid us safe passage
the softest law ripens us in desire's absence

our leaves, the hymn in every silence
sankir skin polished smooth / by olifa and dawning

we, divinity in the becoming
rechristen / palm as psalm / death as familiar darkness.

CHOSEN / GIVEN.

white folks make no promises with their names
can't understand why i refuse to call mia dead while it is still warm
why i won't turn this covenant tombstone / won't choke this song silent

the mark of a colonizer is a short memory
one that erases history / rarely remembers what the people called themselves
only what the land was christened after baptism in their blood
forgets that killing only binds ghosts to the ground they die on

so i could not leave my name if i wanted to
mia is the gift of a feminine body belonging to itself / first / only
it is barbarians gritting their teeth against the settlement
the artifact of mine that will be buried when it is time
or it will not be buried at all.

PEACE OFFERINGS TO A COLONIZER.

after "poutine man makes butter chicken poutine in a crock pot"
by cassandra myers.

food.
the first date / a game of pessoi in the underworld / topical stratum
they always ask to know your favorite dish.
words dying to suck skill from bone
eyes smolder when you sweat like your grandmother's cornbread
claws extend once your veins pump sunday collard run-off
mouths salivate until you volley their query
                    to make or to eat?
brows knit together as they try and fail to explain the difference.
a recipe.

    clothing.
    the first time / a contest of poleis / breached groundwater
    they always wonder aloud why you keep your shirt on.
    speech itching to imprint on skin
    fingertips hesitate against the sapless fiber of your dead
    canines ache when you reveal that which has no english name
    haunches flame possession at your response
        it keeps everything where it's supposed to be.
    ears mistake "body" for "battlefield" and conquer everything in sight.
    a pattern.

        women.
        the first meal with mother / a display of xenia / false-bottom grave
        they always ask to meet her after seeing all there is to you.
        name longing to mark forever
        tongues wet lips when your pidgin tenderizes her for story
        tails flick as they inhale the scent of your inherited girlhood
        knuckles yearn for the evergreen eden of your origin
            you could never know all of her, so none is better.
        hides bristle and singe on contact with the edge of the ownable.
        the hands that made them.

a fishing story.

in this one, i am a sheepshead:
a freak of nature and hard to hold onto.

in this one, you cut open my stomach.
gasp when you find blood instead of sand.

according to the legend, i carry the ground in me,
so it makes sense that i want to go back.

in this one, my skin is just a shawl of scales.
just a raincoat.
just something to keep the salts separate.

in this one, you push your fingertips past my teeth.
i bite down.
my empathy atrophies.
you curse the day you caught me.

in this one, we are not careful what we fish for.
the sea is not a wetter sky.

in this one, i am the deadliest catch.

AMBERGRIS.

all the boys who swallowed left my bed sick   i stared up from the depths of them

a kiss / like shoreline

            with lips / against

                           oh god / yes

            i never had one skim my reef & resurface

a little kobe / gullet the size of sharpness

            a hint of drake / gut to coat the spines in slate

                 gilded / trembling / rostrum

expelled for my trouble   the lesson: call no man like my father

                    right / there

pried up from the ocean floor / feral in the light

                      black market orgasm

      fuck   seaglass fingerprints thirsty for the dune

gasping for breeze through their pores

                        that taste / eternity

so i have not held the peace of absence

we made love like ambergris

mark this body / illegal treasure

                                no more / darling

i need to rest before i take you again.

all the other planets (probe I).

an elegy for retrograde ████████████

mercury.

████████████

    i bookmark it try_not_to_look_away22.

████████████████████████████████

    from prograde / to retrograde / to inertia.

████████████████████████

    this is honest living.

                            venus.

████████████████████████

    i bookmark it rapist_asks_victim_for_second_date18.

████████████████████████████

    my abel horoscope reads like possession.

████████████████

deletes his number / stays friends on facebook / lets our black hole slowly expand.

████████████████████████████████

we're in prograde and retrograde at the same time.

████████████████████

mars.

████████████████████

    i bookmark it ghost_caught_on_camera_at_bar21.

████████████████████████████████

    levitates without leaving.

████████████████████████

    this time, we break / no barstool bones.

████████████████████████

jupiter.

i bookmark it tuesdays_with_no_goddamn_caffeine20.

we used to stain our lips with coffee grounds and silent supplication.

saturn.

like my rings are not retrograding in all the pictures.

my browser immediately gains thirteen shortcuts to the big bang.

uranus.

when the sun sets on earth, it does not disappear from the sky.

i bookmark them both things_that_live_only_in_retrograde21.

laughter progrades out, and for a moment, we are both featureless infinity.

neptune.

██

i bookmark it death_did_not_find_us23.

██

as everything else.

██████████████████████████████

remember that a name has never been a title. that none of us are god enough to survive.

██████████████████████████████

SAPPHO PHAONI (feat. jamilah barry).

don't push me to stay
you know i fall
when you love me this way

all your tricks　　　　　wash up in my throat
　　　　　　　　　　　where you've been since
　　　　　　　　　　　i stopped swallowing low tide

still i know　　　　　　i'd swim through sunrise
　　　　　　　　　　　if you found the right cove

all the games　　　　　let you cry at the cliff of me
　　　　　　　　　　　pray to stave off the end
　　　　　　　　　　　as sand slips through fingers

yeah i know　　　　　　i'm a knot in your net
　　　　　　　　　　　headstone heavy

what i say is final　　　raking regret across your back
　　　　　　　　　　　salinating your bloodstream
　　　　　　　　　　　a red dress rip current

where the love goes i go　with lies burning our lungs
　　　　　　　　　　　build us a lighthouse to abandon

always a break in my fall　when you fall off horizon's edge
　　　　　　　　　　　silk shipwrecked by your scent
　　　　　　　　　　　memory staining my softness

there's no touching my soul
but if the love goes i go
said if the love goes i go

SELF-PORTRAIT OF THE BOI AS AN OYSTER.

a nonet.

open. entice with iridescence.
promise faithfully blooming wealth.
bleed the overzealous hand.
set a price for prying.
prove only the weak
need hunt toothless
beings with
sharp knives
close.

2. semantics.

Oh, mother. It's been so long

since I was the girl in the kitchen

with the dull knife. So long mother

forgive me.

CAMERON AWKWARD-RICH

IDEAL BOUNDS.

[I am] not a man, but a cloud in trousers!   *say it with your whole black mouth.*
      VLADIMIR MAYAKOVSKY   DANEZ SMITH

Life and death appeared to me ideal bounds[.]
MARY WOLLSTONECRAFT SHELLEY

folks frankenstein my speech / graft calm sentences onto aggravated torso /
move into my mouth and immediately reupholster my tongue / draw a chart of
my imagined semantic anatomy / tell me what i must mean when i say / and
maybe this is why everyone hates millennials / a generation stitching together
scavenged syntax by candlelight / using their teeth to punctuate dirty suture
threads / robbing graves to call themselves creators / stopping only to listen / for
the sound of the angels / i mean the mob / over the snuff film screams / and
so they are surprised / when the still-living grammar shakes off rigor / reaches
for the soft throat / an honest question / a bone saw / the deadliest antithesis /
and maybe the monster's sin / is wanting to be translated / exactly or not at all /
or that the cacophony of pitchfork lexicon gives him a fucking headache / and
so he writes himself into a book / where the words make the worlds / and not
the other way around / when did you first commend your spirit / into the hands
of misunderstanding / which psalm taught you to read / this passionate
assuredness as argument / and maybe this is proof that resurrection is hollow
bullshit / and god dwells in the gathering of two or more / half-alive limbs / held
in the genderless / straitjacket of silence / so heaven is / an operating theater /
runway / padded room / pulpit / cockpit / publishing house / a voice that speaks
for me but is not mine.

an interview with olókun.

white person asks me what my pronouns are and berlin conferences my body into parts.
asks me if i recognize my people's viscera.
asks me to give these gendered phantom limbs a name
    that will not trip up the master's throat.
when my tongue refuses,
answers *nigga* like upcycled oppression;
like the whip in my hand;
i remember that even the ways i can call out to this flesh map have been colonized.
that this block has been long gentrified.

white person asks me what my pronouns are and i wonder what it is to pray
    for the fields of these bones without a kokou marching out of my mouth.
i wonder what it is to deny the addict both their substance and their absolution.
to say *the veins of my people carry palm wine and ocean water.*
that *this is the reason our joy lies just beneath our sorrow.*
that *this survival is a revolution and not an accident.*

white person asks me what my pronouns are and turns all the seashells into caskets.
something with a hardness that keeps their ravenous jowls from the meat.
or something to split open and empty into their pockets.
or something to quiet the ghosts of their guilt.

white person asks me what my pronouns are, so ṣàngó awakens
    and we evict them together.
chase them through the sugarcane and cotton prisons they thought could hold òrìṣà.
throw them out of their own front gates.
harvest the sweetness and softness they bled me for.
make an offering of my molasses skin and adorn my own altar.
eat yams until my gender is african again;
until "they" shreds "he" and "she" into "aṣọ oke."
call the new land *nigga.*
share the crop with no one.

LOBSTER TRAP (feat. noname).

a.   "nigga" is a pronoun derived from the american english noun "nigger," a derogatory term used by colonizers to mean "an unwavering darkness."

    ex. *when i go to work, thousands of white people scream the word "nigga" at me.*

        they do not believe lobsters can be born with nightmares of the pot

    ex. *now, the rich niggas is rich niggas with your bread.*

        meat tastes better when the heat-cracked carapace is not your own

b.   the pluralized "nigga" pronoun can be used to reference a familiar group of individuals or a collective identity depending upon its context.

    ex. *niggas broke for a livin' but pray for riches in death.*

        my pockets ain't never right for a funeral / for empty palms
        burnt coffee / bad news

    ex. *what's an eye for an eye when niggas won't love you back?*

        there would be no rainbow without the black from whence it came

c.   invented to describe only a being's phenotypic traits, the "nigga" pronoun, like its predecessor, is not beholden to the gender binary.

    ex. *opportunity knockin' / a nigga just got her nails done.*

        still a stallion in ya hood / steal ya son with these cheekbones

    ex. *nigga just chilling on the couch in a blouse like dave chappelle / be that nigga for life.*

        the baddest bitch be they who hath the sharpest argot between their teeth

d.   since "nigger" descends from the latin adjective "niger," both it and its successor pronoun are black.
  only. always.

    ex. *niggas just carry on / carry on / cry cry, cry, get right back to the money / then carry on / cry cry, cry, hop right back in the pussy.*

    ex. *don't hold me / don't hold me when niggas is dying.*

STRATIGRAPHY.
for the THEM!HOOD.

V. MODERN LAYER

and each time the boi dies
the black word is left to the air again   cry
new kindling in every mouth   love harder
new dances for all the dust

pour one out for 'em
whole hailstorms
than thunder
all the living done together

IV. 2013–2017

their fingertips cartographers of the land
meet red clay in the jaw   flame death
slate lining the rib cage
anoint altars with honest touch

play the dozens with the devil
mans be for everybody
funny box run right over

III. 2006–2012

throat a cavern of infinity   water
hair of pitch-pine smoke
and hands content with emptiness   an appetite
the black word became the boi   ayyyyyye

to a whale
nappy as a briar patch
for every breath

II. 1995–2005

and so this black word spoke itself anew   aw shit.
declared itself a body / a beating fire   go off, nigga.
a burning heart   yo, that's lit.
a brown skin etiology

I. 1994

in the beginning there was the word   oh word?
and that word was black   ayyyyyye
but this primordial black lacked a glyph
a phoneme with no flesh equivalent   damn, that's cold.

BOOKER T. WASHINGTON INDICTS THE TALENTED TENTH.

The hardest thing in the world is simplicity. And the most fearful thing, too.
It becomes more difficult because you have to strip yourself of all your disguises,
some of which you didn't know you had. You want to write a sentence as clean
as a bone. That is the goal.

JAMES BALDWIN

this one ain't for the play-play
        so pack it up if that's what brought you here
ain't nothing funny about this / ragged breath / bloody knuckles / compound fracture
gon' head / write about flowers / sacrifice the stakes
        get ya shit read / or rocked
some of us / carry our homies' loose teeth / in our pockets
know where we'll be buried / that sans serif means a cheaper headstone
        while y'all star-belly sneeches been taking over beaches
those of us without / been watching from dunes
waiting for tidal wave / to show you fools real high ground

i'm convinced / sun could fall from sky shelf tomorrow
        y'all would still ask
where's the heat? / what did we notice? / what work is this apocalypse doing?
so this one's a free verse fuck you / won't make no short lists
        diss track parataxis 'cause i'm sicka y'all
ain't nothing funny about this / sanded word / flat canon / linear assimilation
y'all would braid ya own noose if lynching meant tenure
        mop blood off ocean floor if erasure meant acceptance
gon' head / crack me open coconut-style / steal this south right out my mouth
die mad you can't hack it / ain't built for no crab leg christmas eve anyway

all that meat left on them sentences
        y'all must not be hungry no more

PARABLE OF THE TENANT FARMERS.

That which is below is like that which is above, and that which is above is like that which is below, to perform the miracles of one only thing.
HERMES TRISMEGISTUS

if heaven really is a gated retirement community
the homies and i will spend the next life unionizing the angels.

since a gate is just a wall imbued with discernment authority
not one halo will glow until demands are met.

reasonable triage shift lengths for gate personnel
a system of reporting for incidents with belligerent souls.

comprehensive health insurance including dental, vision, mental, and wing care
a path from part-time to full-time angel.

divine choirs will echo in every room of the landlord's house
we have nothing to lose but our chains.

if heaven really is a high-rise apartment building
the clique and i will declare all the units community property.

should salvation require a credit check or rename itself inheritance
all current terms of damnation will be subject to renegotiation.

though god's image is many, his privilege is few
so if paradise is as private as the dursts' manhattan,

give me and my kinfolk eternal rest in the baseline
cover us with handfuls of dirt and a mouthful of hennessy.

leave this flesh to stage die-ins among earthworms
let niggas go on believing we gon' be alright in the end.

PARABLE OF THE GREAT BANQUET.

an ode to "hungry artist" *by david datuna.*

mere days after we paid our respects to chairman fred
we sat on the stoop slack-jawed as a man ate a $120,000 banana
shook our heads and mused that *the hunger's gonna kill us first.*

sixty-second science class at the self-checkout
appetite / like energy / cannot be lost / only change its form
so when my ~~stomach~~ pockets are empty, i bite the armani-gloved hand that feeds me.

question: if the ancestors were sharecroppers living in eden on credit
what was the price of the apple?

question: if we still have not tired of tilling the fields without tasting the fruit
what is the value of our heads?

in the year of our lord two thousand and nineteen
jesus walks into / a brightly colored spectacle / peels forbidden yield
lets teeth break skin into bleeding / performs a miracle

then smiles as the centurions lead him away from shocked public
peace so still / it shows the cruelty in starving
commands its witnesses to go forth / multiply.

my father might know august wilson.

1. little boy stands by river
both brown opaque beckoning
humid wind rolling down necks
rhythm swelling beneath surface

they converge into one
legend of magnificent banality
story of radiant ordinary
flourish of minor keys

2. black river runs by little black boy
one of them my father
another august wilson
smokestack limbs strain the skyline

they dredge depths under moonlight
seekers of stolen serenity
guardians of dark religion
purveyors of unwritten ritual

3.   boys   stand   black
     rivers   run   black

walter august jesus
be freshwater fence
backwash baptism
brushing silver tide   black

the doctor says

she was gone in the ambulance
i want to ask
if that's why we call it
the dead of night

my mother in the room
my father an ocean away
none of us speak
all of us vain and angry
because what the fuck
did we do all this for

if hope was gone in the ambulance
if *she was gone in the ambulance*
i want to ask
if she knew how hard
we fought to pull her back

would she ever forgive us

all the other planets (probe II).

an elegy for ████████ *my sister brandi.*

mercury.
aries season bursts through skin with blood under its tongue.
████████████████████

my libra appears in the mirror before my barstool bones rise for the day.
waits until after i brush my teeth to ask why everyone blames us. for everything.
████████████████████

disappears in an eclipse when i pretend not to hear her.
i spend the morning meditating naked with an EDM heartbeat to convince her
██████████████

                                                                    venus.
                    a boy who thinks me awan to his cain gores my libra with his horns.
                    ████████████████████████████████████

he says my name / he means it like a prayer / when he leaves me alone in my bedroom.
                    he says he hopes *we can move forward stronger than ever.*
                    ████████████████████████████████

        my libra tries to remember the last time she waned without waxing and cannot.
        ██

            we drink a whole bottle of wine and laugh at how the night sky has no idea.
            ██████████████████████████████████████

                    how we won't be anywhere he can think to find us at all.

mars.
a voice orders guinness at light speed within earshot of my scorpio.
████████████████████████████

when none of her rumble progrades in this stranger's rasp, my scorpio remembers the year
and astral projects.
████████████████

this time, there are no teardrop comets / no sound of stardust retrograding out of flesh.
████████████████

we ask for two fingers of jim beam and smile at how the thing which quells our
darkness has a name that ends in light.

jupiter.
my sagittarius rouses my body in a panic because:
a) we missed our alarms and now we have twenty minutes to get to class.

b) pluto is not a planet anymore / no one seems to give a shit but me.
c) my sister is not alive anymore / no one seems to give a shit but me.
d) today was our sabbath.

saturn.
my mother pretends she cannot see the asteroids [redacted] left my pisces to swim
through.

my therapist recommends that i start "bookmarking" my triggers.

i forget to bookmark drunkenly sending [redacted] flowers / i honestly don't know
what i would call that constellation anyway.
my father calls to say that my sister is not alive anymore / no one seems to give a shit but us.

uranus.
my capricorn and i don't remember my sister's face anymore.

even the image we see is that of the sun eight minutes ago.

we have no idea how the stars decide which triggers we will remember
long enough to bookmark at all.

neptune.
my capricorn and i mix gasoline and frozen orange juice
concentrate in a plastic tub.
██████████████████████████

when nothing happens, wreckx-n-effect reminds me that i am the same
decaying organic matter
████████

i become a gas giant only from a distance. take up all the space i can right here.
██

we have prograde to / retrograde to. there is no space for inertia at all.

dead sibling club.

after lucille clifton.

a sibling once myself
i have a feeling for it
that's why i can talk about environment

my father   last of three boys
never knew
another twelve-fingered conjurer

i   last of two girls
give him the story
a root woman named lucille

somewhere
four severed pinkies finally touch

it all comes down to
presence   absence in the end
we don't call

a single tree   a forest
a single finger   a fist
a single child   a family

the question becomes
what are

                    we now

the new owners have painted the gutters black

my father remembers when this entire block
was a snarling maw of unrelenting forest
begging to be home to something darker than shadow

he and my mother tumbled their wrist bones smooth
spread concrete over freshly cut kudzu
draped naked bradford pear trunks in drywall

bargained with bushkiller over brick
hewed haven for each kind of honeysuckle
naturally the realtor's rechristening omits this

so these gutters end up black
without timbers pulping their spirits free
and siding disintegrating in solidarity

is mine a righteous anger
is blood the only proof of violence

how do i tell our wilderness what we let her become

i open the floodgate

ask what's wrong
he soaks my socks
with a single query

you talk to your mom?

i remember deluge survivors
float to safety
rather than waste precious energy
fighting a ravenous current

not recently.

                              we cling to driftwood
                              desiccated tongues laying
                              salt word on fresh flesh
                              in the temporary stillness

                              she misses you.

                              we watch the minnows
                              avoid our kicks
                              limbs creating small chaos beneath
                              a surface yet unbroken

                              i know.

3. contact.

And I say "Lean in."

"Let me tell you of a wall-less church."

ASHLEE HAZE

BRUNCH.

an aubade for those who do not rise.

my mother asks how i take my coffee now.
sacrifice makes a god of the surrender
not the refuge longing takes in the meantime
so heaven is a white lie ground between my teeth.
    a steaming truth screaming the mo[u]rning awake.

i am descended from women who greet death like brunch.
i do not know if this is bravery or foolishness.
the lesson in leaving love to simmer on the stove
is that the scent often attracts insatiable darkness
    every dish / an ancient meeting place / a taste of here on a plate of after.

perhaps this is the reason i find comfort in black.
close yet unspoken—my sister's alcohol tolerance
papering impulse over hesitance—my grandmother's restaurant etiquette
i have seen enough mo[u]rning to stay dressed for the occasion.
    every sunrise / a party of shallow graves / the singing of two choirs.

heirloom.

the white tee that dem franchize boyz rapped about is
spades tournament crisp and folded in my father's bureau[1]

aaliyah's more than a woman motorcycle jacket is
summer-sun faded but still my sister's size[2]

the pink mink that matched cam'ron's flip phone is
paparazzi primed and haunting my father's closet[3]

nelly's bandaid homage to city spud is
disintegrating rubber stuck fast to our cheeks[4]

[1] the man has everything except two daughters
which means there can be two daughters again until we say so
[2] the man who has everything and his two daughters are the same age
which means they can die at the same time
[3] the man meets an icon with his daughter's name on a beach
which means we talk about them both like they are still here
[4] southern grammar proof that the man had everything and two daughters
which means a scar is better than nothing

dirty magic.

i have not visited my sister
since she became a fixed point
at the mercy of prepositions
a life on the fulcrum of perpetual past

on the highway to someone else's homegoing
offering half-true tales about another ghost
will i ever make it
to the stone altar she now calls home

the season my sister slipped her skin
my father stopped saying her name
buried the incantation as if to keep
the sun off a fragile ancient faith

i have started seeing road signs for dirty magic
since i began approaching her age
the way trees thin themselves between us
has me praying god stays gone til spring

401(k).

a kwansaba for my lungs.

when it's all over / my lungs retire
as birds in south station / expand
like they know they didn't build this nest
but they've learned to love this funny
little bone cage anyway / my mouth doors
open often / remind flesh wings that air
longs to be invited in again someday

TRIBUTARY.

we listen to reggaeton in a sunshower / my black ain't never felt so eternal
primitive humans created the first songs by imitating the birds / that
this gives me hope / my black ain't always sung the melancholy
that the sun was the first bird this black held in its throat

koffee sings about blessings
my black refrains when folk ask where that
this joy was first composed

like this black ain't already hummed the tonic
like we should not sing the loudest chorus
each time the rain does not beckon us back to the sky

my black says ṍya herself taught us the survival melody / that
this is the reason we are still here
that / this good word / it goes like

"excitement: hold your breath
repose: never let them take it"

GOLDEN BOI.

Archeological evidence indicates that writing is a later historical development than spoken language.
DRS. ANOUSCHKA BERGMANN,
KATHLEEN HALL, AND SHARON ROSS

and the boi ain't never felt so ancient
relieved they have not been rendered static by text
thankful they exist only in the mouths of those worthy of the syllables
      only in a sound   an exhale of breath

and here is the first and loneliest freedom the boi comes to know
      the world capsized   the body fell out of its lexicon

then the boi learned to float in a flesh that defies even taxonomy
      to take up space   a single tongue at a time
      to be phonemes with no symbol   save this skin

the boi discovered these bones form legacy with touch
mind / stone put to an apt purpose   heart / kindling for alien fire
              death / a changing of storytellers

and so this golden boi osteology will be how the record remembers them
malleable   shining   ritually surrendered to the earth

JUNETEENTH.

a tattered flag.

> *Small, ordinary acts can be the portals through which meaning is made.*
> DENICE FROHMAN

the man asks "what do you know about freedom?"

> so i tell him how i came out to my grandmother.
> say "i am more intriguing than the violence done to me."
> then i tell him how i wish i could be honest with my mother about my credit history.

or anything that means anything at all.

> and i explain how i talk about my father more than i talk to him
> because "what surprise could a raindrop ever bring the ocean?"
> and i explain how i never wonder if my partner loves me
> when there are biscuits in the house.

only when the man turns to walk away
do i approach

the truth

> is that i was born under a north carolina wind bloated with acid
> where women forge brave lacquered armor of constraint / scabbards full of toil
> slack and useless simplicity clearing loose soil from the excavation
> blood spent lavishly on an empty landscape

> in my house
> in my mother's house
> in my mother's mother's house

a slapdash driftwood body / charybdis waves / guileful / tempestuous

i taught myself to read the gusts by pricking my ears to their howl
thus far the only transliteration that fills this sail of billowing skin

when i say "all the black folks here are smiling"

  i mean "humans are the only species for which baring teeth is a sign of
  benevolence."
  i mean "ain't it funny how enamel ain't bulletproof but we crouch behind it
  anyway?"
  when i say "all the black folks here are smiling"

i mean "all the black folks here are alive
and as soft as water
and eager to stay."

hiraeth (between burgas & varna).

what a safety it is to be told that here,
the worst you can wish on someone is poor health.
shorter years.
less time.

to be told that the harshest curses come from using your mouth to crucify
other people's bodies.
how suddenly no body feels at home between your lips anymore.
how you still choose to keep them astride your tongue rather than beneath your feet.

what a safety it is to be brown here.
to be the color of earth and have them call you soil rather than dirt.
what a safety that the policemen do not reach for their guns at the sight of you.
that there is no mob waiting to kick the breath from your lungs.

here, your identity is allowed to exist unordered.
chaotic good.
the spark of potential between the flints.

here, your body only knows alive.
licks the salt from the air and holds it to your skin.
does not split your wheat from your chaff.
lets the joy multiply the stretch marks.

what a safety it is to be welcome here.
to be a river diverted but not slowed.
what a safety that here is a place you can open without a blade.
like a door rather than a dam.

here, the clicking is the cab driver's tongue sliding gold fronts across teeth.
the clinking is the lev coins mingling in the cup holder.
here, the only destination the man has in mind for you is home.

what a safety it is.

DAP THERAPY.

thích nhất hạnh says *hugging in public is a western practice*
and me and the clique slide off the edge of the earth
cackling over walking tacos in the grass
tongues cumbersome with cartoon cowboy lilt
roasting mans for tryna talk the calluses off dignity and pride

ayo, when's the last time a monk dapped you up?
ayo, how come folks say 'western' when they mean 'colonized'?

thích nhất hạnh says *meditation is an eastern practice*
so me and the homies sail backward along the equator
evicting all the quiet from these temples
throats bubbling over in the chicken joint
asking fam if he knows how long black been conscious of its breath

ayo, pigs must not be pullin guns on black folk in the east.
ayo, ol' dude clearly ain't never quit his job over a hard 'r.'

alligator knuckles / palms worn as dancehall floor / divine lineage of touch
zen is what we name this ritual of survivor's guilt
impermanence spurring every muscle to movement
wild how the grip be different but the message be the same
how these digits be a signal flag that niggas are still here.

ayo, i ain't above you. you ain't above me.
ayo, we side-by-side. we together.

all the other planets (probe III).

an elegy for retrograde & my sister brandi.

mercury.
aries season bursts through skin with blood under its tongue.
    i bookmark it try_not_to_look_away22.
my libra appears in the mirror before my barstool bones rise for the day.
waits until after i brush my teeth to ask why everyone blames us. for everything.
    from prograde / to retrograde / to inertia.
disappears in an eclipse when i pretend not to hear her.
i spend the morning meditating naked with an EDM heartbeat to convince her
    this is honest living.
                                           venus.
           a boy who thinks me awan to his cain gores my libra with his horns.
                 i bookmark it rapist_asks_victim_for_second_date18.
he says my name / he means it like a prayer / when he leaves me alone in my bedroom.
               he says he hopes *we can move forward stronger than ever.*
                   my abel horoscope reads like possession.
       my libra tries to remember the last time she waned without waxing and cannot.
deletes his number / stays friends on facebook / lets our black hole expand slowly.
      we drink a whole bottle of wine and laugh at how the night sky has no idea
                  we're in prograde and retrograde at the same time.
       how we won't be anywhere he can think of to find us at all.

mars.
a voice orders guinness at light speed within earshot of my scorpio.
    i bookmark it ghost_caught_on_camera_at_bar21.
when none of her rumble progrades in this stranger's rasp, my scorpio remembers
the year and astral projects.
    levitates without leaving.
this time, there are no teardrop comets / no sound of stardust retrograding out of flesh.
    this time, we break / no barstool bones.
we ask for two fingers of jim beam and smile at how the thing which quells our
darkness has a name that ends in light.

jupiter.
my sagittarius rouses my body in a panic because:
a) we missed our alarms and now we have twenty minutes to get to class.
i bookmark it tuesdays_with_no_goddamn_caffeine20.
b) pluto is not a planet anymore / no one seems to give a shit but me.
c) my sister is not alive anymore / no one seems to give a shit but me.
d) today was our sabbath.
we used to stain our lips with coffee grounds and silent supplication.

saturn.
my mother pretends she cannot see the asteroids [redacted] left my pisces to swim through.
like my rings are not retrograding in all the pictures.
my therapist recommends that i start bookmarking my triggers.
my browser immediately gains thirteen shortcuts to the big bang.
i forget to bookmark drunkenly sending [redacted] flowers / i honestly don't know
what i would call that constellation anyway.
my father calls to say that my sister is not alive anymore / no one seems to give a shit but us.

uranus.
my capricorn and i don't remember my sister's face anymore.
when the sun sets on earth, it does not disappear from the sky.
even the image we see is that of the sun eight minutes ago.
i bookmark them both things_that_live_only_in_retrograde21.
we have no idea how the stars decide which triggers we will remember
long enough to bookmark at all.
laughter prograde s out, and for a moment, we are both featureless infinity.

neptune.

my capricorn and i mix gasoline and frozen orange juice concentrate in a plastic tub.

    i bookmark it death_did_not_find_us23.

when nothing happens, wreckx-n-effect reminds me that i am the same decaying organic matter

    as everything else.

i become a gas giant only from a distance. take up all the space i can right here.

    remember that a name has never been a title. that none of us are god enough to survive.

we have prograde to / retrograde to. there is no space for inertia at all.

PARABLE OF THE HIDDEN TREASURE.

an aubade for those who are always rising.

on the days my sister's memory is an atrophied muscle
a sax player resurrects the darkest light sample / husks *show me what you got*
becomes the pot howling hymns at the kettle on the Q to church avenue

       family honey-roasts niggas over woolen plats in a black girl's kitchen
       stove hot / tongues sorrel sour / kanekalon viands to emaciated hearts
       metta passes through dap meditation and none of us are tender-headed here

on the days my sister's empathy hangs thick
crab-boil steam clouds ashlee's windows
asia laughs under trees in a prospect park sunshower / superb and inevitable
fire envelops the tip of a blunt rolled with lavender
the grandest branching only complemented by heat

       we two-step across the floor in maya's living room
       transformed and overripe melody / a trap motet with massed strings
       movement one: i forgive her for singing to me in voices not her own

       thank her for the music anyway.

on the days my sister's rings are trophies from a living made by hunting
commerce at an end / the green line sinking into the ocean
movement two: i forgive myself
for marking the change in her tale's narrator

       thank her for lingering to listen anyway.

mini-fridge

(for cassandra, madeline, and joya).

i am the type that has a heart like a mini-fridge.

small; commercial function in compact space.
both cool and ice cold.
sometimes home to other people's leftovers.
sometimes home only to my own.

my heart freezer-burns things that stay too long
no matter how badly i want to hold onto them.
keeps its contents fresh way past the printed expiration date.
won't let me throw out scraps that still feel salvageable.
like the prime rib i made her on new year's eve.
like the half of an omelette in the shape of her smile.
like the lone yoplait cup she promised to come back for but never did.

my heart has filaments that crave the next power surge.
is sometimes tougher than it looks and always tougher than it feels.
has a door that hangs crooked and lets vodka in with the pizza rolls.

my heart tucks the things it can't surrender into its corners and waits for the light to go out.
doesn't discriminate between handmade and store-bought.
has magnets from all the places i've been and dents from all the people i've loved there.
usually takes a day or more to defrost completely.

my heart is a hand-me-down humming toward obsolescence.
a sign of my unwillingness to grow up.
completely unaware of its finite space.
always eager to protect new tupperware.

best of all, my heart stays full. full. full.

(BOI)STEROUS.

an eintou bracelet.

> *The world is not a phantom; it is an assemblage of families.*
> ARCHBISHOP FRANÇOIS FÉNELON

body,
ossuary,
vessel for the next faith,
a totally new unity,
keeper of the bloodline,
holy sundial,
bear fruit.

bear fruit.
hybrid sweetness
for the watching saplings.
birth a name ripe with ritual.
sticky with rebellion.
rambunctious pulp
alive.

alive,
weathered amber
suspends laughter in leaves.
branches whine and whisper pidgin,
grace a staple in dance.
morsel to the
hungry.

hungry
should not exist
if kinfolk have kitchens.
when food is scarce, we eat the mud.
bury the love inside
then wait for it
to bloom.

to bloom,
release the salt.
sift out sting from soil
then water it with tempest wind.
forgiveness lets acid
bathe the new fronds
again.

again
thunder crashes
into the canopy.
lightning makes a meal of the bark;
shed it all. grow it back.
we are more than
body.

Notes

1. articulation.

The epigraph is reverently borrowed from "You're really faithful to your abusers, aren't you?" by Samiya Bashir.

The Giant's Causeway is a promontory of hexagonal basalt columns formed by volcanic activity on the Antrim plateau in Northern Ireland.

Mickalene Thomas: Femmes Noires was a collection of collages and montages by Black contemporary artist Mickalene Thomas housed at the Art Gallery of Ontario from November 29, 2018, to March 24, 2019. It was the first large-scale solo exhibition of her work to be staged in Canada.

"Razbliuto" is a Russian noun that describes the feeling of tenderness for a lost love.

"SAPPHO PHAONI" is the title of Epistula XV in Ovid's *Heroides*. Phaon was an old and unattractive boatman in Lesbos who was approached by Aphrodite (in disguise as a crone) and ferried her to Asia Minor without asking for payment in return. As a reward for this act of charity, Aphrodite gave Phaon an ointment that made his body young and beautiful. Sappho subsequently fell in love with Phaon, but he rejected her after they laid together. Distraught, Sappho threw herself into the Mediterranean Sea to cure herself of her love for Phaon.

2. semantics.

The epigraph is reverently borrowed from "Black Feeling (2)" by Cameron Awkward-Rich.

"IDEAL BOUNDS." begins with quotations from Vladimir Mayakovsky ("A Cloud in Trousers," 1914), Danez Smith ("say it with your whole black mouth," 2018), and Mary Wollstonecraft Shelley (*Frankenstein*, 1818). The poem was written during the 2019 Lambda Literary Writers Retreat for Emerging LGBTQ Voices under the guidance of Danez Smith.

In the religion native to West Africa's Yorùbáland, Olókun is the owner of all rivers and oceans. Depicted with varying gender presentations both in Yorùbáland and throughout the diaspora, Olókun is also the protector of Africans who were carried away during the Maafa, the catastrophe known to African Americans as the transatlantic slave trade.

"LOBSTER TRAP (feat. noname)." begins with a since-deleted 2019 tweet from Noname and features lyrics from her debut mixtape, *Telefone* ("Casket Pretty" and "Reality Check"), debut studio album, *Room 25* ("No Name"), single "Rainforest," and sophomore studio album, *Sundial* ("balloons"). Also included are portions of Noname's verses from Mick Jenkins's "Comfortable" and Ghetto Sage's "Häagen Dazs."

"BOOKER T. WASHINGTON INDICTS THE TALENTED TENTH." begins with a quotation from James Baldwin's 1984 interview with Jordan Elgrably in *The Paris Review*.

"PARABLE OF THE TENANT FARMERS." features the second verse of the Emerald Tablet, one of many texts in the *Hermetica*.

When Georgian performance artist David Datuna attended the 2019 Art Basel exhibition in Miami, he found that a work titled *Comedian* by visual artist Maurizio Cattelan (consisting of a single banana duct-taped to the gallery wall) had sold for $120,000. Datuna subsequently removed the overripe banana from the wall and ate it. When asked at a press conference what motivated this act of defiance, he said, "I call the performance *Hungry Artist*, because I was hungry and I just ate it. The banana tasted good. It tasted like one hundred twenty thousand dollars. The money means nothing, just numbers and papers. It's all about ideas."

My sister, Brandi Corriel Willis, suffered a grand mal seizure in the early hours of the morning on Friday, November 2, 2012. She was twenty-nine; I was seventeen.

Lucille Clifton and my father were born with postaxial polydactyly: an extra finger attached to the pinkie of each hand. Both had these digits removed as infants.

3. contact.

The epigraph is reverently borrowed from "Hymn" by Ashlee Haze.

"GOLDEN BOI." begins with a quotation from *Language Files: Materials for an*

Introduction to Language and Linguistics, edited by Drs. Anouschka Bergmann, Kathleen Hall, and Sharon Ross.

"JUNETEENTH." begins with wisdom offered by Denice Frohman to the 2020 DreamYard Rad(ical) Poetry Consortium fellows.

"Hiraeth" is a Welsh noun that describes the feeling of deep longing for home.

The hugging meditation appears numerous times in the writings of Vietnamese Thiền Buddhist monk Thích Nhất Hạnh. I first encountered it in *How to Love* (Parallax Press, 2014).

"(BOI)STEROUS." begins with a quotation from Archbishop François Fénelon's *Treatise on the Education of Daughters*. The poem was written during the 2020 DreamYard Rad(ical) Poetry Consortium under the guidance of Kamilah Aisha Moon.

Acknowledgments

1. articulation.

"THE DUKE OF YORK @ 5 PM." —*NarrativeNortheast*, Issue 7

"after safia elhillo." —*Gertrude Press*, Issue 34

"razbliuto (between sozopol & nessebar)." —*monster house.* (Jai-Alai Books, 2019)

"A DESCRIPTIVE GRAMMAR ABOUT GENDER." —*the minnesota review*, Issue 96

"BOI FINGERS." —*TWANG Anthology* (2020)

"the body ballet." —*Quarterly West*, Issue 102

"APOTHEOSIS OF THE BLACK BOI." —RADAR Productions' *GLOW* (2019)

"CHOSEN / GIVEN." —*Emerge: 2019 Lambda Literary Fellows Anthology*

"SELF-PORTRAIT OF THE BOI AS AN OYSTER." —*TWANG Anthology* (2020)

"a fishing story." —*The Shade Journal*, 2021 Winter/Fall Issue; *The Slowdown*, Episode 765

2. semantics.

"IDEAL BOUNDS." —*Under the Belly of the Beast* (Dissonance Press, 2020)

"an interview with olókun." —*The New Southern Fugitives*, Volume 3, Issue 3

"STRATIGRAPHY." —Forward Together 2019 Transgender Day of Resilience Art Project

"PARABLE OF THE TENANT FARMERS." —*Homology Lit*, Issue 5

"PARABLE OF THE GREAT BANQUET." —*Recenter Press Poetry Journal*, Issue 3

"dead sibling club." —*Muzzle Magazine*, Issue 33

"the new owners have painted the gutters black" —*The Rumpus* (2024)

3. contact.

"BRUNCH." —*The Offing* (2020)

"heirloom." —*The Rumpus* (2024)

"dirty magic." —*The Rumpus* (2024)

"TRIBUTARY." —RADAR Productions' *GLOW* (2019)

"GOLDEN BOI." —*Emerge: 2019 Lambda Literary Fellows Anthology*

"JUNETEENTH." —*Palette Poetry* (2020)

"hiraeth (between burgas & varna)." —*monster house.* (Jai-Alai Books, 2019); *Cut Poems from Air: Poetry Inspired by Gwendolyn Brooks* (Atrocious Poets, 2018)

"DAP THERAPY." —*The VIDA Review*, Issue 2

"PARABLE OF THE HIDDEN TREASURE." —*NarrativeNortheast*, Issue 7

"mini-fridge." —*monster house.* (Jai-Alai Books, 2019); *A Garden of Black Joy: Global Poetry from the Edges of Liberation and Living* (Wise Ink Creative Publishing, 2020)

"(BOI)STEROUS." —*Litmosphere: Journal of Charlotte Lit*, Issue 3

PENGUIN POETS

PHILLIS LEVIN
May Day
Mr. Memory & Other Poems

PATRICIA LOCKWOOD
Motherland Fatherland
  Homelandsexuals

WILLIAM LOGAN
Rift of Light

J. MICHAEL MARTINEZ
Museum of the Americas
Tarta Americana

ADRIAN MATEJKA
The Big Smoke
Map to the Stars
Mixology
Somebody Else Sold the World

AMBER McBRIDE
Thick with Trouble

MICHAEL McCLURE
Huge Dreams: San Francisco
  and Beat Poems

ROSE McLARNEY
Colorfast
Forage
Its Day Being Gone

DAVID MELTZER
David's Copy:
  The Selected Poems of
  David Meltzer

TERESA K. MILLER
Borderline Fortune

ROBERT MORGAN
Dark Energy
Terroir

CAROL MUSKE-DUKES
Blue Rose
An Octave Above Thunder:
  New and Selected Poems
Red Trousseau
Twin Cities

ALICE NOTLEY
Being Reflected Upon
Certain Magical Acts
Culture of One
The Descent of Alette
Disobedience
For the Ride
In the Pines
Mysteries of Small Houses

WILLIE PERDOMO
The Crazy Bunch
The Essential Hits of
  Shorty Bon Bon

DANIEL POPPICK
Fear of Description

LIA PURPURA
It Shouldn't Have Been
  Beautiful

LAWRENCE RAAB
The History of Forgetting
Visible Signs:
  New and Selected Poems

BARBARA RAS
The Last Skin
One Hidden Stuff

M.S. REDCHERRIES
mother

MICHAEL ROBBINS
Alien vs. Predator
The Second Sex
Walkman

PATTIANN ROGERS
Flickering
Generations
Holy Heathen Rhapsody
Quickening Fields
Wayfare

SAM SAX
Madness

ROBYN SCHIFF
Information Desk: An Epic
A Woman of Property

WILLIAM STOBB
Absentia
Nervous Systems

TRYFON TOLIDES
An Almost Pure Empty Walking

VINCENT TORO
Hivestruck
Tertulia

PAUL TRAN
All the Flowers Kneeling

SARAH VAP
Viability

ANNE WALDMAN
Gossamurmur
Kill or Cure
Manatee/Humanity
Mesopotopia
Trickster Feminism

JAMES WELCH
Riding the Earthboy 40

PHILIP WHALEN
Overtime: Selected Poems

PHILLIP B. WILLIAMS
Mutiny

MIA S. WILLIS
the space between men

ROBERT WRIGLEY
Anatomy of Melancholy and
  Other Poems
Beautiful Country
Box
Earthly Meditations:
  New and Selected Poems
Lives of the Animals
Reign of Snakes
The True Account of Myself
  as a Bird

MARK YAKICH
The Importance of Peeling
  Potatoes in Ukraine
Spiritual Exercises
Unrelated Individuals Forming
  a Group Waiting to Cross